Food Groups

Meat and Protein

Lola Schaefer

www.heinemann.co.uk/library
Visit our website to find out more information about Heinemann Library books.

To order:
☎ Phone 44 (0) 1865 888066
Send a fax to 44 (0) 1865 314091
Visit the Heinemann Bookshop at www.heinemann.co.uk/library to browse our catalogue and order online.

First published in Great Britain by Heinemann Library, Halley Court, Jordan Hill, Oxford OX2 8EJ, part of Pearson Education. Heinemann is a registered trademark of Pearson Education Ltd.

Editorial: Diyan Leake and Kristen Truhlar
Design: Joanna Hinton-Malivoire
Picture research: Melissa Allison
Artwork: Big Top
Production: Duncan Gilbert
Originated by Modern Age
Printed and bound in China by South China Printing Co. Ltd

ISBN 978 0 431 01522 4 (hardback)
12 11 10 09 08
10 9 8 7 6 5 4 3 2 1

ISBN 978 0 431 01529 3 (paperback)
12 11 10 09 08
10 9 8 7 6 5 4 3 2 1

British Library Cataloguing in Publication Data
Schaefer, Lola M., 1950-
Meat and protein. - (Food groups)
1. Meat - Juvenile literature 2. Proteins - Juvenile literature 3. Cookery (Meat) - Juvenile literature
I. Title
641.3'6

Acknowledgements
The publishers would like to thank the following for permission to reproduce photographs: © Getty Images pp. **15** (Stone), **28** (Stone), **29** (First Light); © Harcourt Education Ltd/Tudor Photography pp. **4**, **9**, **12**, **19**, **21**, **23**, **25**, **27**; © Heinemann Library p. **26** (David Rigg); © istockphoto.com pp. **13** (Paul Cowan), **16** (Achim Prill), **17** (almond, Hasan Kursad Ergan; pistachio, Ahmet Cuneyt; walnut); © NaturePL p. **7** (Philippe Clement); © Photodisc p. **22**; Photolibrary pp. **10** (Foodpix), **11** (PureStock), **14** (Anthony Blake), **20** (Foodpix); © Punchstock p. **8** (UpperCut Images); © Still Pictures p. **6** (Steven Kazlowski); © Stockfood UK pp. **18** (Glenn Peterson), **24** (Food Collection).

Cover photograph reproduced with permission © Photolibrary.com (Brand X).

Every effort has been made to contact copyright holders of any material reproduced in this book. Any omissions will be rectified in subsequent printings if notice is given to the publishers.

Disclaimer
All the Internet addresses (URLs) given in this book were valid at the time of going to press. However, due to the dynamic nature of the Internet, some addresses may have changed, or sites may have changed or ceased to exist since publication. While the author and publishers regret any inconvenience this may cause readers, no responsibility for any such changes can be accepted by either the author or publishers.

Contents

Some words are shown in bold, **like this**. You can find out what they mean by looking in the glossary.

What are meat and protein?

Meat is the parts of animals that people eat for food. Most meat is full of **protein**. Some other foods besides meat are also packed with protein.

All of these foods are full of protein.

Meat and protein are one of the **food groups**. People also call this group "meat and beans". You need to eat some protein foods every day as part of a good **diet**.

Where meat and protein foods come from

Cattle, sheep, pigs, chickens, and turkeys are raised on farms. People eat the meat from these animals. Fish are caught and eaten. Wild animals like duck and deer are hunted for their meat.

People go out to sea in boats to catch fish.

Beans grow in pods on bean plants.

You can also get **protein** from plant foods. Beans and peas are grown in fields. They have protein inside of them. Nuts and cheeses also have protein.

What meat and protein foods look like

The meat that we eat can be different shapes, sizes, and colours. Meat and fish can be red or white before they are cooked. They often change colour when they are cooked.

These foods have a lot of **protein**.

Beans and peas are small and almost round. Beans can be green, white, red, or black. Peas are green. Nuts are different shades of brown. Each nut has its own shape.

How meat tastes

Chicken and turkey are meats that have a **mild** flavour. Lamb and duck have a stronger flavour. Many people add **seasonings** to meats.

Barbecued meat tastes good with sauce brushed on it.

Salmon is a fish with a strong flavour. It has many **nutrients**.

Fish is also a meat. Some fish have a mild flavour, and some have a strong flavour. Some people add butter to fish when cooking. Others pour sauces over the fish.

How other protein foods taste

Dried beans and peas have little flavour. People put them in sauces, soups, or rice. They then add **seasonings**.

This person is adding beans to vegetable soup.

Cheese is a protein food that is easy to prepare.

Nuts are crunchy and have a strong flavour. Eating a handful of nuts is a good way to eat **protein**. Some cheeses have **mild** flavours, but others are **tangy**.

Why meat and protein foods are healthy

Protein builds muscles. It keeps your heart and lungs healthy. Protein is used to make hair, skin, and bones. It also helps your body fight germs.

Eating fish is a great way to eat protein.

Meat and protein foods also have other **nutrients** for your body.

- B **vitamins** help make energy and build strong blood.
- **Iron** carries oxygen in the blood.
- **Magnesium** builds bones.

How much meat and protein do you need?

Most children 5–10 years old need 3–5 servings of **protein** each day. A serving could be a piece of chicken or a small hamburger. One serving could also be a tuna fish sandwich.

Meat can be served with vegetables to make a healthy meal.

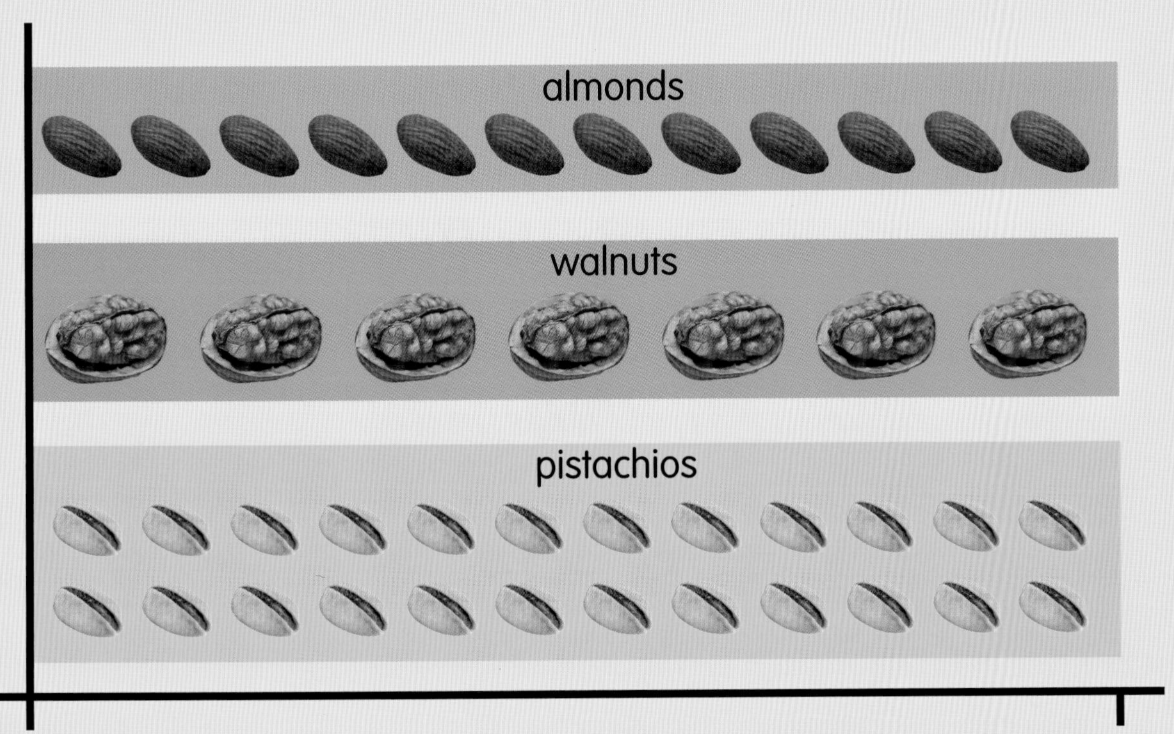

Look at this graph to see how many nuts equal one serving of protein.

An egg could also be one of your servings of protein. A tablespoon of beans is another serving of protein. A tablespoon of peanut butter is a serving of protein.

Meat and protein foods to eat for breakfast

You can eat a scrambled, fried, or poached egg for breakfast. Eggs add **protein** to your **diet**. You can also have a small piece of bacon or sausage.

Eggs are easy to make and full of protein.

A bagel with smoked salmon is a healthy and filling breakfast.

At breakfast, you can add a handful of nuts or seeds to your cereal. This is **lean** protein. Or you can have a bean and cheese **tortilla**.

Meat and protein foods to eat for lunch

A turkey sandwich can be a healthy lunch. Soups made with beans or **tofu** are another great way to add **protein** to your **diet**. A grilled cheese sandwich has protein.

Tofu is made from soybeans. It tastes good fried together with vegetables.

Quick and easy tuna salad

Please ask an adult to help you.

- Drain the tuna.
- Add the mayonnaise, vegetables, and black pepper.
- Mix well.
- Serve and enjoy.

You will need:

- 175 gram can of tuna
- 1½ tablespoon (tbsp) mayonnaise
- 1 tbsp diced cucumber
- 1 tbsp diced red or yellow pepper
- 1 tbsp diced radish
- 1 tbsp chopped tomato
- black pepper

Meat and protein foods to eat for dinner

Many people add grilled chicken, turkey, or fish to a large salad. Some put meat in pasta. Other people eat omelettes.

Enchiladas are made from **tortillas**. They can be filled with beans to make a meal full of **protein**.

Cheese mini pizzas

Please ask an adult to help you.

- Butter the muffins and place under the grill until lightly browned.
- Spread the tomato purée over the tops.
- Sprinkle the cheeses over the tomato purée.
- Place the mini pizzas back under the grill until the cheese melts.
- Serve and enjoy.

You will need:

- butter
- whole wheat English muffins
- tomato purée
- grated parmesan cheese
- grated cheddar cheese

Meat and protein foods to eat for snacks

One of the easiest snacks is **protein**-filled cheese and crackers. Hard cheddar cheese is healthier than soft cheese spreads. Hard-boiled eggs can also be prepared and kept in the refrigerator for a quick snack.

Hard-boiled eggs are a tasty protein snack.

Snap and crack snack

- Mix all the nuts and seeds together in the ziplock bag.
- When you are feeling hungry, take a handful and enjoy your quick snack.

You will need:
- 1 tablespoon (tbsp) of walnut halves
- 1 tbsp of almonds
- 1 tbsp of peanuts
- ½ tbsp of pumpkin seeds
- ½ tbsp of sunflower seeds
- a ziplock bag

Nuts and seeds are a healthy snack that will give you a lot of energy.

Keeping meat and protein foods fresh

Meats need to be frozen or kept in the refrigerator. Never eat meat after the **use-by date** on the package. Eating meat that is too old can make you ill.

Read the food labels on meats carefully.

Nuts can be stored in the freezer or refrigerator to keep them fresh.

Store dry beans and peas in air-tight containers. Keep them in a cool, dark place. Beans and peas lose their **nutrients** when they are kept for more than two years.

Do meat and protein foods alone keep you healthy?

Meat and **protein** foods are good for your body, but you need a healthy **diet** of many foods. You also need at least four big glasses of water each day. Drinking water helps keep your body healthy.

Eating a healthy meal with family and friends can be fun.

Exercise builds up muscles and helps you stay healthy.

As well as healthy foods, your body needs regular **exercise**. You should try to get a little each day. You also need to get plenty of sleep each night. Sleep helps you stay strong and well.

Glossary

cattle cows or bulls that are used for meat and dairy products

diet what a person usually eats and drinks

exercise physical activity that helps keep a body healthy and fit

food group foods that have the same kind of nutrients. There are five main food groups, plus oils.

iron mineral that helps blood carry oxygen through the body

lean having little or no fat

magnesium mineral used to build bones

mild not sharp or strong in taste or odour

nutrient substance (such as a vitamin, mineral, or protein) that a person needs to stay healthy and grow

protein nutrient in food that gives the body energy and helps it grow

seasoning ingredient used to flavour food. Salt and pepper are two seasonings.

tangy sharp or unusual flavour, taste, or odour

tofu healthy food made from cooked soybeans

tortilla flat, thin cake made from cornmeal or wheat flour

use-by date date on food packaging that shows when it needs to be eaten by

vitamin nutrient in food that a person needs to stay healthy

Find out more

Books to read

Go Facts: Healthy Eating, Paul McEvoy (A & C Black, 2005)

Look After Yourself: Eat Healthy Food!, Angela Royston (Heinemann Library, 2004)

What's on Your Plate? Breakfast, Ted and Lola Schaefer (Raintree, 2006)

Websites to visit

www.5aday.nhs.uk
Click on "Fun & Games" and then "Did You Know?" to find out amazing food facts.

www.childrenfirst.nhs.uk/kids/health/eat_smart/food_science/index.html
Click on the meat and vegetable protein on the tray to find out more about why these are good for you and how many you need to eat each day.

www.nutrition.org.uk
Click on "Cook Club" for some great recipe ideas.

Index